THE 2 OF ME

THE 2 OF ME

Sarah McChristian

authorHOUSE®

AuthorHouse™
1663 Liberty Drive
Bloomington, IN 47403
www.authorhouse.com
Phone: 1-800-839-8640

First published by AuthorHouse   09/30/2011

ISBN: 978-1-4634-6020-4 (sc)
ISBN: 978-1-4634-6019-8 (ebk)

Library of Congress Control Number: 2011915074

Printed in the United States of America

This book is printed on acid-free paper.

…ENSIGHTFUL, LIFE CHANGING, ABOUT A REAL PERSON

Edward C. Tucker, PhD
Detroit, Michigan

Understanding the emotional capacity and how to manage human responses to negativity should be a part of educating our youth today. As an educator for 30 years, I recognize that this understanding, as part of the school curriculum, would facilitate the building of student character, student morals and a student appreciation toward humanity.

Sharon Bryant Phillips
Author and Spanish Teacher

This book is powerful, in that it illustrates a glorious work manifested in the author's life. This inspired work is truly a testimony of a mother's love for her daughter. Many of the words in this book have empowered me. Most assuredly, it will have a transforming effect upon anyone who reads it.

Cassandra G. Turner, MLS, MA
Adjunct Professor, EMU

Very enlightening…a good guide for life experiences. It inspires positive thoughts and solutions.

Lois Hilfer, LVN
Arcadia, CA

THE BEST PHILOSOPHY:

Mature adults need to know…

"THE MOST IMPORTANT YOU"

Discover yourself.

(Relieve that fear, depression and stress)

FACTS THAT HELPED ME TO MOVE
MY THINKING
WITH PERSEVERANCE
TOWARD PERFECT PEACE.

I learned how to look and feel good;

So can you!

Check out…

THE 2 OF ME

By Sarah McChristian

A Physical Introduction

Surprisingly, I have learned how to love all kinds of people; some of whom, with which I did not even want to associate. I can remember attending the funeral of a man who was my neighbor, as well as, the husband of a co-community, club member. That man had tried to get me to sneak out on a date with him. Please don't misunderstand, that early in my life; I certainly did not love the deceased man (after I found out what he was trying to do) but I truly loved his wife and their family. I wanted so to tell them during his funeral not to be so mournful, because I had learned of his dishonesty . . . but of course, I could not speak about such truth.

There have been a series of unusual circumstances that have caused me to become a very different person than I ever thought that I would ever become. These changes took place over a period of many years. I would pick up the sign of a distant light shining somewhere inside of me, only to learn that the light represented a person with whom I had not wanted to associate with to whom I was being mysteriously, intellectually drawn toward. High School had made me into a student accepted only for my music talent, because primarily; I had been a social outcast due to the fact that I happened to be an African-American, prior to Civil Rights. Amazingly, an English teacher (who had never been my personal instructor) came to me one day while I was working at school on Hall Duty, and stated that she had read a paper that I had written. She stated that my writing was enjoyable; therefore, she said that she wanted me to enter a National, High-School, Essay Contest. I don't remember what I wrote about, but that teacher edited my paper and I won the contest. The prize was a course in Radio Speech at Michigan State College. Subsequently the following summer, I spent living away from my parents for the first time on campus in East Lansing. It became the **only** lengthy period during my years in High school, that I really enjoyed life. I assumed it was because I was able to easily befriend the other student winners whom I suspected were the "cream" of all students in my age group.

Actually, High School was the age at which I began to seriously examine myself. The wonderful part of my childhood resulted from attending a very rural, one-room schoolhouse. It was amazing, but in retrospect the few attending students had made me feel like a family member with them. There had been **only one** incident where a family that moved into our neighborhood from Tennessee enrolled their school children who chanted, "Eeny, meany miny-Moe, catch a nigger by his toe, and if he hollers make him pay, a hundred dollars every day." My school-mates warned these kids to never repeat such. When they ignored this warning, my school-mates pushed these Tennessee kids into the thinly, iced ditch on the side of the road which caused the ice to break and wet their feet. These children had to run more than a half mile with ice cold feet before reaching their home. The next day when they returned to school (and thereafter) they became family with the rest of us. I had pledged with two Grade School friends (with whom I had sung for many years in a trio) that once we became adults, the three of us would all become professional singers.

It was High School that made me hate school. I began to be depressed. I had to project myself as normal. I learned how to appear as a happy person but I realized that although I wanted to be a part of my High School Class, I was not socially accepted because I was a different color. African-Americans did not accept me because they said I was trying to be white. I decided they also were prejudice; I was merely a product of my environment; therefore, I must become totally independent of both **black and white** people. My Dad and my friend, Mary (my age, who lived across the road) were my only friends. I loved my Dad because he always made me think about how to solve problems. He would say, "Answer A leads to this result; Answer B will bring this result; and C will bring this result. I would choose answer B, but **you** have to make your own decisions which is like making your own bed because **you** have to sleep in it." I would **always w**ant to select whatever option my Dad had chosen. He always gave me such understanding. My Mother, on the other hand, would always **demand** that I do whatever she said because . . . **she** said so! I would then think, "Wait until you're not looking you dictator!" She was a real <u>challenge</u> in my life! Fortunately, I did not have to relate to her during the week because she worked at a city facility where she had to live to remain eligible for employment. She came home only on the week-ends. My Dad would telephone me to let me know he was on his way to pick her up to bring her home. This meant I had to make sure **everything** was as spotless as possible. My Mother complained if **anything** was out of place! Moreover, she subjected me to unfair treatment, not only because she was a dominant-perfectionist, but she would fiercely discipline me for whatever she imagined that I had wrongly done. I recognized that her terrible behavior was due to the fact that, she had only partial hearing in one ear, but more importantly she had very little formal education. She hounded me continually to recognize that she expected me to project to all of our white community that . . . **our** black family did not agree with their negative, black stereotypes!

Meanwhile little incidents like riding on the high school bus . . . I would be made to feel invisible because I was sitting next to a classmate, while another classmate standing in the isle were planning a pajama party right over my head for that evening, and **I was not invited!** I remember going out into the hall at school one day to find out why so many kids were laughing so loud, only to discover that at the bottom of the list of "who's going with whom to the Prom" my name was listed as having been invited by the school dork. These kinds of humiliating incidents were regular occurrences for me. My escape plan was to marry at an early age to gain my independence from my mother and my school.

I had been the roller skating partner of a black graduate from the same high school who lived a few miles from where I lived. I was truly pleased to know that he wanted to marry me. He purchased me a tiny diamond engagement ring (which the kids at school joked that it must be a Birthday present from my parents) and I was pleased to learn that my parents liked this young man and agreed that we could marry. We had a beautiful church wedding that summer.

I put my confidence in my husband. We lived with my parents while we built a beautiful home on property next door that my Dad gave to us. Our first born child was an unbelievably, beautiful girl. My life really started to change when I was selected while singing in a talent show in Detroit by a gentleman who wanted me to be a featured vocalist with his trio. At first I was suspicious and asked my husband to go with me for the audition. I landed a featured, vocalist career with The Casey Jones, Instrumental-Vocal Trio. I was so proud to have such a glamorous career and realize that I was probably making more money than my former classmates. I wore beautiful, formal clothes and jewels; publicity photos were posted outside each club. I sang my heart out every night with a style of expressive blues that had people crying in their beer. However, I could not ingest more than two alcoholic drinks without becoming very ill so . . . I remember giving my alcohol to an alcoholic barmaid (who thought that I was the best thing since chocolate cake) and I drank a fruit-lemonade that looked like a Tom Collins. I realized that it would a "conflict of interest" for me to refuse the customer gift of a free drink! Each time we left the stage for a break (from 9PM-2AM with 40 minutes on stage and a 20 minute break each hour) and we came to sit down, a customer would have bought us a round of drinks so that we would sit with them. They wanted whoever was entering the club to see them sitting with us. (It was only after I had received spiritual eyes that I understood what the wise, King Solomon meant when he stated, "All is vanity and vexation of the spirit."

My nine-month old daughter needed surgery to correct her ruptured navel. I was completely torn to have to leave her reaching for me from the hospital crib, as I was leaving. She was crying for me to stay with her. However, I was under contract for a career I had dreamed of most of my life. We had to head for the city in which we were engaged; but at that moment, I realize the Mother half of me had won. I would not sign another contract; I would give up show-business to become the mother that I should be.

A few years later, I visited Sarah Vaughn back-stage where she was cutting out her daughter a bathing suit to sew as a gift for her. This famous singer looked into my eyes and stated sadly, "My daughter's Birthday is in a few weeks and this is as close as I can be to her." I felt sorry for this famous woman because I understood, "you can't have your cake and eat it."

Infidelity had broken into my marriage of eight years which made me feel so violated, I finally decided to get a divorce. I even appreciated the opportunity to befriend a person who would be my second husband before our divorce was final. I had longed for so many years to be appreciated by a gentle, loving and kind person in a non-argumentative relationship. I did not even care that he was an alcoholic.

My next child was a delightfully, brilliant, sweet baby-boy. When he was nine months old he began to toddle. My husband and I were shopping with him when suddenly, he fell in such a manner that he twisted and paralyzed the nerve that controlled his diaphragm. He stopped breathing! My husband went to apologize to the clerk who was showing me new shoes. The clerk yelled. **"Get him to the hospital!"** I was already running to our car with one shoe unfastened. A station wagon filled with a driver and four children pulled up next to our parked vehicle. The driver who noticed the limp body of my son offered to take me to the hospital. **However,** a very definite, authoritative voice (inside of rne) demanded that I not get into that station wagon with those people! I knew my husband was unfamiliar with the city of Ann Arbor. The University of Michigan Hospital, at that time, was the closest hospital. I was being given instructions by that same inner voice teaching me how to breathe for my son. When I looked up . . . because my husband was speaking in a tone of voice I had never heard him use," Where is the hospital wife?" I was shocked to see him running through red traffic-lights on campus! I'm sure it was an adversarial, familiar-spirit that the bible speaks of that spoke and told me that my son was going to die. It said, "You tried to save that kitten when you were 8 years old that fell into the giant can of milk on your Dad's farm; but **he died; didn't he!"** **Yes,** the kitten died so . . .

. . . in a strange way, this familiar spirit made my memory recall that each time I breathed for the kitten, milk bubbles would come out of its nose and its body would feel as thought it was living. But, when I would stop breathing for it, its body would become stiff like a dead body. My son was reacting in the same ways . . . when I breathed for him (mucus would come out of his nose) and he would feel alive, but when I stopped breathing for him, his body would become stiff like a dead corpse. I refused to respond to this spirit or to my husband demanding, **"Where is the hospital?"** I knew I must keep breathing for my son but, occasionally I knew I needed to look up to point in the direction of the other smaller hospital on the other side of town. Meanwhile . . . . I was sarcastically thinking that, we could not even get a police escort to the hospital because we were not making an illegal turn! Suddenly, my husband slammed on the brakes to keep from hitting a police car that was parked at the emergency entrance of the hospital! This action caused my fingernail to press against my son's tongue which must have shocked him into crying. I jumped out of the moving car (my shoe still unfastened) but knew I would not fall even though I was running into the hospital emergency entrance, as fast as I could while carrying my son. I thought . . . if the hospital staff asked me for insurance papers, I will scream loud enough for all patients in that hospital to hear me! Rather, in a matter of moments, a doctor took my son from my arms and rushed him into an examining room; immediately, three other doctors surrounded the examination table. I heard a woman sobbing like you hear actresses perform in those dramatic, television soap-operas; then, and I realized it was me who was sobbing! The doctor declared that my son's body temperature was low, but that was understandable, under the circumstances of his not having breathed on his own for such a long period of time. **I had been supernaturally given instructions concerning how to keep my son alive!** He would live! He would be fine.

I stayed at home with my toddler. I had to make myself not follow him around all day. I took a class in CPR (cardiopulmonary resuscitation). I learned that the nose should be held closed while you breathe for a non-breathing person. However, once my son was able to walk steadily . . . I realized that if I was ever going to have another successful career, I needed to return to school. I chose to clean houses to pay for tuition and other school expenses. I worked for two professional bachelors who lived in town. One was a Horticulturalist and the other was a Math Teacher. Both gentlemen enjoyed spending time with me to hear about my show-business experiences; so I would make lunch for them on the days that I worked for them. One such a day, the Math teacher hurriedly entered the front door, somewhat out of breath and stated, "Sarah you've got to hear this recording that was made by the Moog Synthesizer. (This was one of the first music computers.) This recording is perfect; it has not been touched by human hands!" He came into the kitchen and sat down at the table with the two of us. The computer voice was singing, *Are You Sleeping, Brother John*. The pitch, the tempo, the meter, everything seemed perfect. The English language seemed to be the only imperfection in the recording. I wondered might it be possible for computers to take over show-business. "This is going to be your new competition," the Math Teacher jokingly commented. I knew this was my cue for a socially polite laugh (and I did laugh) however, I had read so much science fiction as a young person, **I truly felt intimidated by his remark!** It must have been the feeling of ambiguity that I experienced, from my external laughing, but at the same time, hating, from within a deep, visceral area . . . the concept of machines taking over the field of music performance, that **subsequently, suddenly projected me right outside of my body! I was literally beside myself!** I could hear myself laughing, and at the same time, I could see my physical body sitting right beside me . . . laughing; and I could also see the two men sitting at different angles, at that kitchen table with me!

Right through the house wall came a fascinating light-sphere that looked like the sun, would look through colored glasses only it was the size of a basketball. It paused, several inches right in front of my out-of-body eyes! Strangely, the former, somewhat familiar, authoritative voice asked me, "You want to know what this object that you are looking upon happens to be, don't you?" Of course, I wanted to know what this fiery energy-ball might be! "You are looking at, **pure, unadulterated fear!**" was the response that I was given. "If you become fascinated with this spirit, it can shape-shift, cover you, and you would **never** be able to find its borders! You would **never** be able to control your body again . . . these men would have to take your laughing body to a Mental Institution!"

Immediately, I accepted the warning, and immediately stopped looking at this fascinating, energy-ball. Immediately, thereafter; I was elastically sprung into my physical body right through the side where I had been sitting! It seemed as if I had been outside my physical body for several minutes, however, when I looked into the eyes of the person facing me (seated on the other side of the table) I realized that I had only been outside of my body for a nanosecond . . . between chuckles. I never told these men what had happened to me that day, but I did begin to understand that outside of the physical/ time realm there exists more than the wind that we cannot see. It truly is amazing how humans coexist with indefinable numbers of living, as well as, non-living entities that we never even consider. That day, I also had learned how different time is . . . outside of our physical existence.

I read as many books, as possible, by people who wrote about their out-of-body experiences. I remember one man who had numerous adventures outside of his body. He stated that when he was asleep and dreaming, in his dream, when he realized that he was dreaming, he had an ability to travel anywhere he would choose to go. He could travel in space above the earth or, down into the ground below the surface of the earth. Reading about his out-of-body travels was completely captivating. He stated that he had to coin the term, "skyreting" to describe flying throughout our solar system. He said he on that kind of adventure when there appeared a room into which he entered and discovered many white-robed, white-bearded men in a meeting. They immediately asked him to leave. He obediently left the room. He stated, near the end of his book, the very last time he was able to skyret . . . he was flying at a tremendous speed through outer space when two giant angels suddenly stopped him in mid-air by each of them placing a hand on each or his shoulders; They both yelled at him (as they both pushed him with much force in the opposite direction) **"You are not supposed to be here!"** He was elastically sprung back into the side of his body (where he belonged) back into his bed. He said knew that he was not able to **ever** have anymore such experiences. He said he knew that next time he would be outside his body he would be dead. I thought . . . I never want to be outside of my body again until I am dead!

The Director of a Drug Treatment organization that consisted of an Out-patient Methadone Clinic, an In-house Treatment Facility and a Prison Psychological-testing Referral Program, stated he hired me to work in all three programs because he was impressed by my educational background. The Physician responsible for my initial, In-service Training, told me to spend at least an hour a day looking out of my office window to learn about the people moving about in the inner-city neighborhood because I could never learn these behaviors from reading a book. I carried a case-load of clients for whom I was responsible for their individual, as well as, group-therapy drug-counseling. It didn't take long for this change in my lifestyle to give me a need to be able to psychologically-vent such extreme . . . never experienced behaviors that I encountered on my new job while daily listening to the shocking stories that drug addicts shared. My husband refused to want to hear about this unusual behavior because he said he had to grow-up living with and listening to drug addicts! Therefore, I chose to lunch each day with another Social Worker who had an office in the same building in which my office was located. She had been hired by the Federal Government to hypnotize her clients out of their sub-cultural behaviors. Her clients would not have been able to pay for Psychological Counseling; neither would they have wanted to spend the necessary therapy time. They were also granted the privilege to pay for her services with a government subsidized program a fee amount on a sliding scale related to their income. This confidential Counselor would patiently listen to me vent the amazing emotions that I felt from listening to my many, drug-subculture clients; after which . . . she would share the stories that **she** had encountered from people with every kind of unimaginable, antisocial behavior. She was always the winner. She counseled pedophiles, exhibitionists, kleptomaniacs, schizophrenics, etc. (I learned many years later that, the entities that bring about most of these kinds of abnormal human behaviors are merely old, Familiar Spirits that even understand our ancestral weaknesses.)

I had begun to feel a need to seriously study the bible so, instead of taking the required class in Philosophy (my first two years in college) I had received permission from the Dean of Schoolcraft College to be a guest at Madonna College and take a class in Old Testament History. Unfortunately, I was unable to even afford the tuition of that expensive school! Subsequently, I had to take the Philosophy Class at Schoolcraft. I convinced myself that I could tolerate **any** class for one semester by simply regurgitating whatever the Professor wanted me to write for a term-paper. Needless to say, I was shocked to learn that my assigned professor informed our first class meeting that he was an atheist, a Deweyite, and a pragmatist. He further informed us (a powerful lesson) that the real test of one's personal philosophy (in practice) would be advantageous if we . . . knew how to disagree agreeably. I thought to myself, his statement certainly sounds like a true concept, but . . . I'm certainly not going to test it with any religious principles. I was **determined** I would do **nothing** to risk my GPA in a challenge with this atheist professor!

I began to be carried into a new realm of comprehension. I had lost an argument with the Lord when I learned He wanted me to write a term-paper for my professor, as well as for me to learn a lesson. **"What about my GPA?"** I demanded. "The lesson is logic, and you can impress him by using much of the psychological terminology that you have learned from your extensive study in the field of Psychology," was my answer. "You have to show me what to write!" I said with disgust. "You can title your paper *An Application of Emotions* and I will teach you the reasons how, as well as, why the human emotional capacity should be maintained." I clearly recall at the end of that semester, the professor calling me up to his desk and telling me, "Your paper is one of the most logical papers that I have ever read; it is well written; I'm giving you an A on it and an A in my class; but I don't believe a word of it!" I thought, "Thank you God, I'm out of here!"

(Amazingly, many years later, I was able to write a book from that term-paper that teachers and counselors told me should be in every school system in the United States. It is titled, *SMART IS AS SMART DOES, Emotional Self-help for Young People.)*

My most lengthy employment has resulted from two State Jobs. Next to my longest State employment resulted from two, different positions that I held with the Michigan

Employment Security Commission. While working as a Job Counselor, one of my responsibilities was to prepare women to work in previously held, high-paying, male positions at a huge, General Motors Plant. (I could feel the resentment from the men who worked inside that plant while I was on assignment filming for the presentation I had to prepare to teach women how different the Plant environment would be compared to what probably had been their usual school or hospital job environments.) My other position was as an Alien Certification Specialist. I was placed in that position to insure that workers could not be brought into this country at lower wages if there was an American looking for the position that a foreigner was being considered for. However, once MESC staffs had most of the people in Michigan working, **we lost our jobs** (we were laid-off.) The Secretary of State Department had to hire 50 of our group (of State, laid-off staff employees) for 50 perspective, Secretary of State Office Management positions because our employee, State—ranking was at a higher level than that of their Secretary of State Office Clerks from which they normally promoted to those Office Managers positions. Not only was this a State, employee motivational objective, but it was extremely more easy to train these perspective managers from a staff who understood the functions, as well as, the laws associated to this kind of an office business. I could not even identify one kind of vehicle, license plate from any other kind of vehicle, license plate!

I passed all of the State tests and was given assignments throughout much of the lower peninsular as an assistant manager and a substitute manager. Finally I was given my own office to manage. State officials paid me to take some college-level, managerial classes.

One evening I was laying on my stomach on my bedroom floor studying with my cat sleeping on my back, when I paused for a moment to contemplate if I wanted to give up my career as a Social Worker to remain an State Office Manager. I glanced at the hundreds of books upon the many book shelves in my bedroom. I heard what had been the familiar, authoritative voice ask me (in a very loving manner) "Have you read **My** book?" I knew I had no excuse for not having read the bible . . . I could not say that I did not know how to read or that . . . I had not had enough time. I was just so grateful that I was alive when I was being asked this question. I could have been dead; facing the Lord when HE asked this question! Immediately, I pondered upon the fact that **HE is an <u>all</u> or <u>nothing-at-all</u> God.** I truly wanted to give all of my life to HIM, I didn't know how and the only people that I knew who I believed were true Christians and truly serving HIM were non-smokers. I was smoking a cigarette. If I was to learn from those people, I could not smoke. I had unsuccessfully tried many time and different ways to stop smoking. I demanded, **"You have to take these cigarettes out of my life!"** My desire to smoke immediately left; it was if I had never touched a cigarette in my life!

The next day at work, when I mentioned I was no longer a smoker, a co-worker blew smoke in my face stating, "Oh you'll be smoking again in a few days." Forty years later, I have never touched another cigarette. I recall lying on the sofa for three days in my Family Room while the Lord gave me instruction on how to change my active vocabulary. He showed me that when we say that someone is nice, it could mean that we are tolerating that person or we love that person.

HE showed me how to let my "yeas be yea, and my nays be nay." My visiting Brother informed my Mother about this behavior of mine so, she rushed to visit me and stated, "If she saw me without the same clothes that I had worn for those three days, she would burn them." (They both thought that I had "gone-out on the deep end.") But I knew I was being given an understanding related to learning how to exemplify truth. Wow! My hunger for truth was beginning to be satisfied!

In retrospect, I knew that I had become a person that I had not wanted to be. I wanted to change my life because of:

The collection of revengeful events that I had tried to plot or scheme; the laws that I had deliberately broken; my jealous resentment; my verbal tearing down of another person with unkind words about the past, all of which I had to add lies to make myself look like a better person than I was: wow . . . all of this behavior weighed heavily upon my heart. I had done so many things that I had previously said that I would <u>never</u> do. I sensed that I had been psychologically effected by man's "games of competition" along with my innate, egocentric need to look as successful as possible . . . I had learned to compete, whenever necessary, within my world. I exaggerated who I was. I wanted to live a life of truth but I could not. I remember winning a trophy for my High School in a District Talent Contest. My piano teacher told me that I could be dramatic by throwing my hands up into the air after completing each of the many, repetitious arpeggios within an exciting composition that I could easily memorize. My audience (through a lack of musical knowledge) would definitely be impressed. My friend who studied much harder than I had, had to **read** a Bach Fugue that she had selected (written with counterpoint, which meant, when playing it, you must use both sides of your brain simultaneously.) She was crying back stage because she had made a mistake during her performance and had to start over before completing her presentation. I won the contest but, I certainly had begun to understand that human competition, whether it is exercised within beauty or sports could not be truly fair. (Look at how much more has been accomplished by the United States and Russia working together in space than when they were involved in the space-race.)

Games of co-operation have brought us much greater achievements than have games of competition. Whenever I have seriously listened to that Important Voice giving me supernatural instructions, I was never in trouble. For example, I was told I would be delivering a friend's baby . . . so I took a course in Mid-wifery from The Motor City Mid-wives. The baby was born on a day when the outdoor temperature was many degrees below zero. Road Services stated that they did not care if you were a Doctor, you would have to wait your turn. The Mid-wife who had been selected to deliver that baby could not start her car, so I had to deliver the baby.

As I mentioned earlier in my physical introduction, my Mother's cruel behavior made me spend much time studying in many different areas within the field of Psychology. Many years prior to the recent crimes committed by young people, I recall having read Daniel Goleman's book titled, *Emotional Intelligence.* This extensive, research scientist was able to prove that EQ (our emotional quotient) is a better gage than is IQ (our intelligence quotient) in determining the likelihood of the success of an individual. He stated near the end of his book that, younger and younger children would become involved in more and more serious crimes. It is unfortunate that many people do not realize that emotional self-control is a life-long necessary human task.

Daniel Goleman posed the crucial question. "If we don't begin to teach emotional self control to our young people **now,** when are we going to begin?" Let us begin to examine a major factor related to human possibilities by looking at the all important human emotional capacity for which each of us are given the life-long responsibility to maintain.

The Emotional Capacity

Some people are not taught that humans have a life-long job of maintaining their emotional capacity in a way that will be to them . . . most advantageous. Many people believe that they have the **right** to experience any feelings that come their way because they do not recognize the many disadvantages that negative emotions can and do bring to the human body/mind (a two-way connection.) The reason we know that there is a limit of negative emotions that a person can experience is the fact that, ultimately, a negatively, unmaintained, emotional capacity can be the demise of the individual. We can become so depressed that we commit suicide; we can conjure so much hate against a person or persons that we murder (knowing the consequences could be our execution) or we might become so frightened that we have a heart-attack and die. Over a longer period of time, various, physical ailments can also be contributed to habitual, faulty thinking.

It is natural for a newly born infant to experience much, negative emotions simply because of its lack of knowledge. The baby does not understand that a stomach cramp is indicating the need for food. Psychological, as well as physical, nurturing is necessary to teach humans how to adjust to a co-existence of life with others. We are born with a selfish (egotistical) nature and we want as much of everything that we appreciate for ourselves. The Field of Psychology considers this innate behavior as a self-preservation mode of the human species. Subsequently, we are socialized to share with others but, the self-preservation mode remains constant throughout life because of the many, constant human, physical demands.

The most socially, vulnerable period in human, emotional development is when an individual reaches the onset of the "self-actualization" process, i.e., they move away from being "others" directed to become "self" directed. A problem that easily can exist during this period is caused by the fact that one's ego makes us prefer to ask advice from our friends (who know no more than do we) instead of seeking advice from those who have effectively led us to that crucial, developmental, point in life. If we have not the understanding of how easily one can be mislead at this point, we can be lead away from all of our aspired goals by believing that we can do something that is contrary to what we have been taught, so then subsequently we believe we can get away with behavioral actions that can secretly be to our advantage. Prisoners have shared with me that they felt they were getting away with an advantage until the police put handcuffs on them. Most prisoners stated it had been when they were Middle School age that they first began to go astray.

Lessons in ethics, character education, and philosophy is certainly valuable in preparing the human mind to make good decisions, however, an understanding of "God's law of love" is the **only** preparation a person can have that will allow them to experientially, understand the essential, spiritual aspect of the human being.

Vital Emotional Limits

The fact that our emotional capacity is limited is exemplified (by the previously mentioned fact) that if improperly maintained, i.e., filled with mostly negative emotions, it can position our behaviors to become extreme enough to result in the demise of our physical existence. Therefore, it is vital (a life and death issue) to realize that the more positive emotions that are maintained within our emotional capacity, the less room there is for the negative emotions and vice versa.

Human behavior, can vividly, more easily reflect the **opposite end** of the positive (love related) emotions . . . those emotions that are hate and fear related. There are two, prominent periods within the human life experience which relate mostly to negative emotions. We should only want to experience the one that we are all subjugated to and that is . . . We are all **filled** with negative emotions when we are born. Thereafter, early in life we begin to establish personal taste preferences beginning with a preference for certain foods; however, parents or guardians have to teach us how to accept the foods that we do not like. Egocentrism makes it necessary for humans to be taught (actually socialized) into learning how to share. The only **other** time in life an independent adult would experience a domination of negative emotions would be **if** that person would have <u>failed</u> to <u>learn</u> to <u>properly maintain their emotional capacity</u> (allowing enough negative emotions to dominate that capacity) so that they would be at a serious risk of losing their own self control and even facing the possibly of experiencing a mental disorder. Unfortunately, most parents or guardians do not emphasize how important it is to recognize that emotional self-control can be either an advantage or a disadvantage in defining who we are.

Remember the two year old (that we have all witnessed) become excited because another two year old has come to visit? They are both pleased to stand, face and look into each other's eyes. The visitor picks up one of the many toys that are displayed on the floor. **However,** the two years old, toy owner immediately snatches the toy from the visitor . . . "No! Mine!" he yelled! "**Yes**," said the parent or guardian, "We must learn to share." Parents teach us how to share and how to accept some things that we do not like but most people do not realize how very dangerous negative emotions can be.

The next page presents an emotional quick glance. Although this fact is not considered within the field of Psychology, the listed, negative emotions were given to mankind by the sin of disobedience brought on by the free-willed, first humans. After examining an emotional quick glance, let's examine who I am, in other words, who we became.

Emotional Quick Glance

POSITIVE: LOVE RELATED EMOTIONS

- Love: acceptance, friendliness, trust, kindness, affinity, devotion
- adoration, infatuation, agape
- Enjoyment: happiness, joy, relief, contentment, bliss, delight,
- amusement, emotional pleasure, sensual pleasure, thrill, rapture,
- gratification, satisfaction, euphoria, whimsy, ecstasy
- Surprise: amazement, wonder, astonishment

---

*NEGATIVE: HATE/FEAR EMOTIONS

SHOCK: FRIGHT, DREAD

DISGUST: CONTEMPT, DISDAIN, SCORN, DISTASTE, REVULSION

SHAME: GUILT EMBARRASSMENT, GLOOM, REGRET, HUMILIATION, MORTIFICATION, REMORSE, CONTRITION, JEALOUSY

SADNESS: GRIEF, SORROW, GLOOM, SELF-PITY, LONELINESS, DEJECTION, DESPAIR, SEVERE DEPRESSION

ANGER: FURY, OUTRAGE, RESENTMENT, WRATH, VEXATION, ANNOYANCE, IRRITATILITY, HOSTILITY, HATRED, VIOLENCE

FEAR: ANXIETY, APPREHENSION, NERVOUSNESS, WORRY, MISGIVING, EDGINESS, DREAD, TERROR, PHOBIA, PANIC

Who Am I?

There is a life/death reason for those who have not been "born again" to understand human spirituality because we cannot accomplish such without help because, we are continually subjugated to the never ending demands of our flesh from the moment of birth. The innate rule of "self-preservation" (needs) merges with our ego (desires) to make us on guard in all relationships within our environment. We prefer to feel comfortable. Unfortunately, our personal tastes (likes and dislikes) cause us to mentally collect some erroneous stereotypes which eventually bother our consciences to the point of causing us to personally examine our personality with the purpose of occasionally "cleaning house," in other words, make the necessary, personality corrections that correctly, improve our character. Finally, when the three processes of physical, psychological and intellectual growth have impacted us at high enough levels, we are provided with a good understanding of personal advantages, as well as, an understanding of personal disadvantages. When we are able to examine the causes of justice and injustice, we begin to search for absolute truth. Our research begins with an examination of governments (and laws) then we look into the field of Philosophy to try to understand what is right and what is wrong thinking, as well as, what is right and wrong behaviors. Intellectually, we try to understand a difficult family member by studying the field of Psychology but, we soon recognize that this field primarily categorizes mostly abnormal and deviant, human behavior.

Animals appear to behave in ways that signify that they do what they were created to do . . . . but man? Can I ever become the wonderful person that I project myself to be to others or, must I continue to be the secret hypocrite that I am? It is certainly logical for me not to have confidence in others as I learn to unmask their hypocrisies. I have the choice to either accept my character flaws as "normal" or; I need to know if it is possible for humans to be good because, I have certainly tried, and I have always <u>wanted</u> to be good. However, many years in the early part of my life, I was the proud, self-asserting, goal-seeking, (outwardly-appearing successful) person. People usually have to be brought low by failing circumstances in their lives to begin to reason about how to become the person that they <u>truly</u> want to be. I heard a European woman explain that the people of her Nation were subjugated to have lived in a war-torn country. She stated that during that time, the churches were filled with people helping people . . . when bombs were falling everywhere out of the sky! She said the dying person in the church next to you would give you their last container of drinking water. However, when the war was over, and everything had been rebuilt, the person who was beautifully dressed, sitting next to you in church would not even speak to you. We have heard it said that, we learn when we are in the valley and not when we are on the mountain top. Cataclysmic events do make us stop to reason. Why was I born?

The collection of the supernatural experiences that happened to me, that I have shared with you . . . finally, made me study the bible to learn from the Master Philosopher, His intentions of how humans are to development to become spiritually mature, in other words **perfect** (the ability to disagree agreeably.) Hummm . . . I learned this fact from an atheist professor 40 years ago! However, most people do not understand the facts associated to how that we can <u>easily</u>, mistakenly believe that we are good.

THE HEART

King David (a man after God's heart) finally recognized that he had allowed the physical lust of his body to cause him to commit violent crimes against others and violent crimes against himself.

In the 55th chapter and the 10th verse in the book of Psalms, David seems to plead when he asks God to, "Create in me a clean heart, O God; and renew a right spirit within me." This verse is often taught in church. However, one of the greatest prophets, Jeremiah (while witnessing the practiced, idolatry and apostasy of the Hebrews which brought them much destruction) gave the human species a verse that is completely **vital** but . . . **not** taught by those who are supposed to be responsible to present "the truth to the captives!" Jeremiah seems to have understood that because Adam and Eve partook of the fruit of "good and evil" they removed human beings from the perfect loving, emotional realm in which God created us . . . into the "sin" (negative) realm of deceit, lying, hiding, etc, emotional state that we must overcome to be allowed to dwell with God. He states in Jeremiah the 17th chapter, verse 9 . . . "**The heart *is* deceitful above all *things*, and desperately wicked: who can know it.** If we speak with a gentle, soft voice and sacrificially spend time helping others, our hearts tell us that we are good. Jesus clearly states that kind of thinking is deception of the heart. If Jesus, as a human on earth (and completely subjected to the authority of His Father) **refused to call Himself good** . . . how can we be so blind as to believe that we are good! The 19th chapter of Matthew in the 16th verse, the rich young man called Jesus good. Jesus stated (in the following verse) "Why callest thou me good? *There is* none good but one, *that is* God: but if thou wilt enter into life, keep the commandments." How often are we taught to "love our enemies?" Has your congregation ever prayed for Bin Laden? What was Jesus teaching in Matthew 5:43-45? **<u>Are we the children of God if we remain disobedient to this teaching?</u>**

Ye have heard that it hath been said, Thou shalt love thy neighbor, and hate thine enemy. But I say unto you, Love your enemies, bless them that curse you, do good to them that hate you. And pray for them which despitefully use you, and persecute you. That ye may be the children of your Father which is in heaven: for he maketh his sun to rise on the evil and on the good, and sendeth rain on the just and on the unjust. (Matthew 5:43-45)

Only two churches out of seven are acceptable to God (in the book of Revelation.) I believe this fact could be associated to the fact that; because we were instructed to imitate Jesus; and Jesus spoke openly more about hell than of heaven, the church problem could be associated to the fact that . . . we seldom hear that "three letter word" spoken in the churches today.

The Spiritual Heart

The spiritual aspect of a human consists of many similar parts that comprise the human, physical body. Before we can understand the spiritual aspects of a person, we must recognize the truth of God's word. Until that happens, we are, as is mentioned in the bible, with eyes, but cannot see, with ears but cannot hear. In other words, we are prisoners of logic and psychological reasoning. We are completely unaware of the eternal, spiritual aspect (that is more of who we are than a mere body) that makes it necessary to know God personally to be instructed by him regarding the secrets within his word so that we can understand that **his** truth was given to us (signifying **his** love) to guide and protect us. Unfortunately, God is viewed by non-believers as the "cosmic killjoy;" when in fact, he is just the opposite. He does not force his "lessons of eternal life" upon us because he wants us to love him because of **who he is.** Only when we sincerely ask **his** forgiveness for our wrong, past lifestyle, and then request that he comes into our spiritual hearts to guide us in the understanding of his word and then; we surrender to the superiority **of his** Holy Spirit, can we see the need for obedience to **his** word. Then, his word must become our operating manual otherwise; we become lost in the strivings of the many processes of living. **He** gave us **his** word to **protect** us through "the valley of the shadow of death," (life) so that we can have a **much better existence,** following which (after this life) we can live eternally with **him. His** word (John 3:16) let's us know that: God so loved the world that he gave his only begotten Son that whosoever believeth in him **should not** perish, but have everlasting life. If we ignore this bible verse, essentially, we are illustrating that we believe our self to be wiser than our creator. The life/death question then becomes, "Should a person who has been given the opportunity to exist but, willingly chooses to ignore the vital instructions on how to make it possible to live the **better life eternally,** be granted such a privilege?"

Bible dictionaries classify the human soul as being the spiritual mind of an individual. It is compared to one's ego in the natural sense. The self-centered, character of the human species remains faithful to a personal philosophy of relativity because every person has the innate, egotistical function classified by the field of Psychology as "self-preservation." Throughout life, personal achievements boost the ego of an individual to such a level of pride that, it can remain difficult for a human to admit being guilty of disobedience associated to what was taught during childhood as erroneous behaviors. Therefore the human soul, (our spiritual mind) in each of us, remains as inactive as does our unused, spiritual eyes and ears until we begin to examine life.

According to the bible, the beginning of our wisdom can be associated to moving beyond the concepts of relativity if we carefully examine the scientific-beauty of all creation. Man remains incapable of creating any living or growing thing. Humans re-create. Furthermore, collectively, man has achieved in print, beautiful forms of government with laws however, in practice, throughout every society, injustice prevails. Therefore, righteousness, justice and truth **must be sought** to be found. The only sensible explanation for its planetary absence is explained in the bible. God's law of agape (unconditional) love can only be experienced within our spiritual hearts (after our rebirth into our brand new, spiritual self) which will allow us to give dominate control over our material (fleshly) systems to our new-born, spiritual hearts to let it be subjugated to the new indwelling of the Holy Spirit. Only **then** can we worship God in spirit and in truth.

Reasoning

The following biblical facts will reveal much of the reasoning associated to God's will, His word, and His ways to those who do not know Him. First of all, God is love. However, His love is agape love, meaning it is unconditional. This also means that **all** of His personality characteristics (therefore **all** of His deeds) are associated to this fact. All of His creations reveal His love. God is omnipresent, meaning He is everywhere. God is omniscient, meaning He is all knowing. Any and all beings who love certainly appreciate when their love is reciprocated. Reciprocated love cannot be forced. Therefore, God (the Creator of **perfect everything and perfect everyone)** gave man and woman a free will; the right to make their own behavioral decisions. However, on the sideline, the great enemy of all, Satan was able to convince Eve (the first created woman) to disobey God by enticing her to partake of the tree of good and evil and then she convinced Adam (the first created man) to do likewise. This disobedience brought the consequence of sin-death to all future mankind. The price of sin is death; therefore, God sacrificed an animal (the first blood, sin sacrifice) to make a body covering for the newly, sinfully disobedient Adam and Eve who had suddenly felt, shamefully naked.

The Holy Scriptures explain how God chose the small nation of Israel, with whom He would have communion so He could teach a group of people to have the ability to teach other people about himself. This was another merciful gift from God because within a time period of between 1,000 to 2,000 years, man had become so extremely confused and very evil, that their lifestyle demonstrated a desperate need to understand how they should live . . . subsequently, they had even created many false gods. God began by teaching Israel how to gain a consciousness of sin, by teaching them to conduct animal sacrifices to **cover** their sins. The **present** covenant between God and mankind came when God sent his perfect, Son Jesus (who chose to obediently sacrifice **His perfect blood)** for **all** who are willing to accept this free, beautiful gift to <u>**remove**</u> **their sin debt.**

This act was the beginning of God establishing his Church (that is not made by human hands) that consists of the body of obedient believers where Jesus is the chief cornerstone. According to the 28th chapter in the book of Isaiah, God's Church is made of a measuring line of God's justice (a horizontal line) that is perpendicular to His righteousness (a vertical plum line.) This solid and true building is a structure that will be able to withstand the "hail" and "storms" of the coming judgment. However, many individuals will chose to go their own way instead of God's way . . . (that behavior simply exemplifies that they feel that their decisions are smart; smarter than God?) Furthermore, it is impossible for any human to exist in the presence of a holy, righteous God unless we have learned to surrender our egocentric desires to the control of the Holy Spirit gift that we are given when we accept Jesus as God's own Son. That superior, supernatural power is what we need for **all** of our guidance, healing and comfort. Those who have experienced this loving-power do so by always praising and thanking God! Let us get an understanding of how God's supernatural love compares to the natural, limited love of man.

Love

The most important, as well as the most difficult, emotion to define is the emotion of love. There is *impersonal love* defined as love expressed by a dedication or commitment to projects pertaining to causes, or noble objectives related to people, animals or beneficial, planetary systems. Then there is an enormous range of *interpersonal love* among human relationships. Interpersonal love can be defined by close ties of an individual to family or friends. One of the most powerful love expressions is that chemical bonding, mammalian drive that can lead to a physical attachment.

Wikipedia defines many cultural definitions of love from around the world from Persians, Chinese, Japanese, ancient Greeks, Turks and Romans. However, there has always been the need for cultures to teach the difference between love for "me and mine" as compared to love for "all people." Self-centered, humans have always found the Philosophy of "love for all" (the selfless kind of love) more easily spoken than it can be accomplished. Furthermore, there has always been the confusion of defining lust as love.

World Religions have always defined love as a means of establishing purposeful bonds between human beings. Some ancient religions subjected leaders into fertility, and sexual rituals. However, Buddhists and Hindus associated the sensual love as simply an onset to understanding how to love with compassion and mercy. Islam teaches the concept of a **universal brotherhood** as being related to Allah who is "full of loving kindness." Arab Sufism is called "the religion of love." The Universe is merely a reflection of God who is the Lover, who is loved, and is called the Beloved. Man is to learn to love humankind by an appreciation of all of creation.

The God (of Christianity) is explained in (I John 4:8) as **Love**. When the power of love is examined in the bible, it is proven as the <u>greatest</u> <u>existing</u> <u>force</u>. The love of Jesus was certainly exemplified by his giving his life to pay the sin debt for all who believe he was sent of his Father, God to pay the sin debt. When we examine human emotions it becomes apparent that before sin came into the world (everything that

God created was good) Adam and Eve (even with a free-will) were perfect before they disobediently partook of the "Tree of Good and Evil." When examining human emotions, we can recognize all of the goodness related to "positive-love" emotions, while on the other hand, we can see how sin relates to the "negative-hate/fear" emotions.

Unfortunately though, we take it for granted that because the emotional capacity of a new-born is all negative (due to their lack of knowledge) it is **normal** and therefore acceptable for humans to always be partially negative. However, the power of the Holy Spirit was given to mankind (those, who accept it) to teach us how (to be again, as we were when man was first created) so as to become acceptable to live with our, perfect, holy, Father God.

The following page is a love-gift to help young, inexperienced people to understand the misunderstandings related to love.

by Sarah McChristian

Dear, dear Reader

Please remember that most of the parables that Jesus taught were related to planting and reaping. Likewise, I will share with you the following love lesson:

There are three kinds of love. 1. Agape (unconditional) the kind of love that is described in the bible as "stronger than death"(only achieved through the power of the Holy Spirit.) 2. Eros is the kind of love that was created for the purpose of procreation. It is a powerhouse. The bible explains (because of a chemical/spiritual bonding) that a man will leave his parents and cleave to his wife so that ultimately, the two shall become one flesh. The world, via stories and movies, promotes a "touch and feel" relationship (including passionate kisses and embraces) between individuals who have experienced the mysterious chemical exchange that initially takes place between two person who have begun a mutual interest in each other. 3. Last and least is the love that humans naturally experience that is called Phileo which is a love for family and friends.

Please remember to properly understand the definition of Eros, it must be viewed as "beautiful but dangerous." Hollywood has made love into a game of physical lust, therein is the danger because the embraces and kisses condoned by the world lead to the kind of intimacy that God intended <u>only for marriage.</u> (Matthew 19:5) I say, "Touchy-feely leads to the beddy-weddy; <u>even if you are not married!</u>" In a future phase of your life . . . when you recognize an interest in a person of the opposite sex; please remember that, that person must be a true believer in Christ Jesus <u>and</u> you both must allow agape love to rule your relationship with the power of the Holy Ghost (the only force stronger than Eros.) Then, God will truly bless your relationships. Until then . . . . I pray that <u>all</u> of your relationships remain fruitful. (Colossians 1:10)

Purpose by Sarah McChristian

Those who refuse to believe in anything supernatural have no spiritual eyes or ears. They are totally unaware that, more important than the physical body that we devote ourselves to (which is temporal) is the eternal, spiritual, most important aspect of the human being. Therefore they cannot either understand the process of "being born again." Only individuals who have become burdened with a history of behavior that they had previously declared would not represent them as a person; and then, if they experience a contrite spirit (one of sincere remorse) and subsequently seek assistance to overcome being responsible for such adverse behavior . . . and finally if they call upon the Lord, HE will enter their life and cleanse their sins; and open their spiritual eyes and ears. Only **then** can they understand how valuable God's plans are for mankind.

The honorable and highly rated field of Psychology promotes the concept that, it is normal for humans to have to overcome the total abundance of negative emotions that fill the infant emotional capacity at birth, via parental nurturing and education. These concepts are accurate but totally limited. When we only have concern for who we are, without an understanding of whom the Creator **intends us to be**, we can never expect to move out of the realm of the life-long, good-evil, human, emotional conflict. One of the most amusing analogies defining man is found in the book of Isaiah that explains when man is proud of himself; he is likened-unto an ax bragging about having cut down a tree. Everything that we have is a gift; therefore we need to try to understand why Jesus was given to mankind by our Creator. Otherwise, we may continue to believe that we evolved from primates, even though we have never seen a transitional ape-man. The Genome (DNA) Project (deciphering the human code) has totally invalidated the antiquated, Darwin theory. However, man keeps looking outside of the book of Genesis to explain how and why life came about. It is hard to believe that there has ever been an unwritten code. Scientists continue to work at striving to decipher the human, DNA Code. So . . . let us examine mankind by looking at the perfect Economy established by our perfect Creator to motivate us to choose which kind of eternal existence we should prefer.

God's Economy

God's economy could not be more motivational! When we examine the difficulties in establishing a program to "move the masses" (much of mankind) into a desired direction, we must admit that God's economy of **heaven or hell** is the perfect solution.

Unfortunately, politics can carry believers within a nation into national pride along with empty religious rituals. Whenever we try to fill the space within our emotional capacity that was designed for HIM alone (the area for worship) we are guilty of idolatry. Many people try to place people, accomplishments, or material wealth instead of God within the space reserved for HIM within each of us. God is, and has the right (as our creator) to be . . . a jealous God. Therefore, God promised to punish nations for faithlessness in HIS word (behavioral immorality) **and** idolatry (the worship of things or people instead of God). Furthermore, in these last days, many individuals are guilty of mixing psychology, ethics, philosophies, as well as, personal preferences with the word of God.

The word of God declares that religious groups will move into that direction. In II Timothy 4:3, 4 the Bible states: "The time will come when they will not endure sound doctrine; but after their own lusts shall they heap to themselves teachers, having itching ears. And they shall turn away their ears from the truth, and shall be turned unto fables."

Jesus spoke more about hell than he did about heaven. Do our religious leaders follow HIS example today? The prophets and ministers in the past did so . . . but today we don't hear anything that might upset the listeners. We are presented with only lessons pertaining to *the goodness of the Lord's blessings*, and encouragement from messages relating to *the love of the Lord for HIS people*. Is a half of a picture the truth? Paul said in 5th verse of II Timothy, "But watch thou in all things, endure afflictions, do the work of an evangelist, make full proof of thy ministry."

Throughout the word of God HE declares that HE will lift up believers who are humble. We are to be **extractors** and **reflectors** of **HIS righteousness**! God will one day, judge all people, and cast Satan with all of the wicked unbelievers into his perfect prison of hell. This act of justice will allow Him to bring all of the true followers into His established new heaven and a new earth where the **true believers/ teachers** can dwell with HIM **forever in His perfect places!**

Recently the Lord informed me that I would be willing to die for my enemy. I thought, "who is my enemy?" Then I remembered a woman who walked up close (face to face) with me and told me that she hated me. "Yes," I thought, "I would ask you Lord to strike me dead in front of her if I thought that she would look at my dead body on the floor and think . . . "I wish I could be a true believer like Sarah was!" Then her soul would be saved from hell!

"Remember 40 years ago how you cared more about your GPA than you did about your Philosophy Professor's soul? See how far I brought you," was my Savior's lesson that day.

Look back and see where HE brought me from!

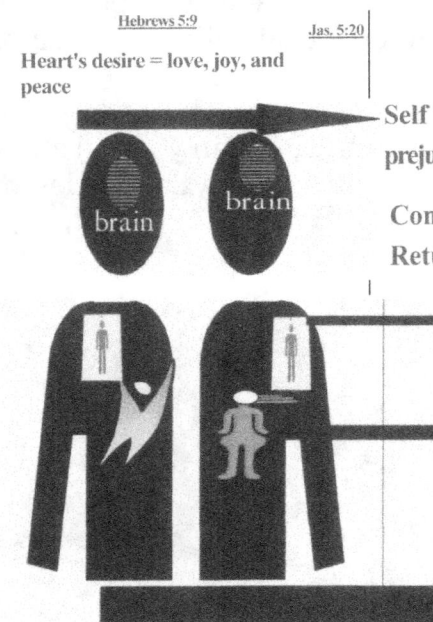

Hebrews 5:9

Heart's desire = love, joy, and peace

Jas. 5:20

John 11:16 Thomas called Didymus means twin (Greek)

We are all twins (temporary) flesh and (eternal) souls. Gen 2:7 Created from ground; returned to ground.   Mark 3:29

Self protection, selfishness, greed, (sin) likes/dislikes prejudices, reason, plans and logic Jeremiah 17:9 Gal.5:17-26

Conviction unto salvation. Hunger/wisdom of God's word. Return love to God. Love all humans including enemies.

Ability/desire to do Jesus' work. Love, joy and peace from the Light of the Holy Spirit

John 12:36

The human soul with the "spirit" (brain of the soul) Ability to unconditionally love and worship. John 4:23

Ongoing, daily demands of the dominant human flesh learning from the world. 1 John 2:16, 17

male   female

But seek ye first the Kingdom of God and his righteousness; and all these things shall be added unto you. Matthew 6:33

3-2=1

Mat. 13:1   Mat. 25:34-40

When we surrender to the superiority of the Holy Spirit; God gets all of the credit for our changed behavior!

The only way to become one with Christ as HE is one with the Father. (John 17:21)

Senior Lessons

The previous page is a hypothetical look at the invisible, human body capacities illustrating what is spiritually possible when we surrender to the Holy Spirit, once we have accepted this wonderful gift. Otherwise, we don't have the power to "love our enemies" or even come close to being obedient to the word of God. Many years ago I met an older woman in my church who became a mentor to me. She insisted that I become involved in Prison Ministry. The first day that I was being introduced to prisoners in a court-ordered, boot-camp, prison-alternate facility, I learned that I would have contact with these men only twice before they were released. "What can I teach these men that they will never forget when I will only have contact with them twice?" was my question of desperation to the Lord. (These men are "doing time" because they "wasted time; was **my** lesson) so "Teach them "about time" from the dispensational time chart that you have been studying," was my answer. Yea . . . I was able to draw on the classroom blackboard (a similar copy located in the back of this book) what I titled, *God's Calendar*. These prisoners were trained as are military men so they were the best students that I have ever had. They realized that if they could not complete the several weeks of training, that they would have to go to prison; so they were very highly, motivated students. I explained to them that time is set into eternity as our planet is set into space. They kept thanking me for the lesson. They said they had been in and out of churches much of their lives but had never heard that lesson. One day, as my mentor and I were waiting for our identity to be checked (sitting in our vehicle outside the prison gates) my mentor asked me, "Sarah, do you know what I want?" I was thinking, what could she want (**as old as she was**) that she had not had by now? (I didn't make this statement because I had too much respect for this wonderful woman.) My mentor stated, "I want to be standing in the front of a line of people that is so long that you can't see the end of it; and I want Jesus to be introducing me to each person by name and letting me know that **I** was the person who had told them about Him!" That statement changed my life! I thought to myself, if I have anything in that round ball on the top of my shoulders . . . then this will have to be **my** new goal in life because everything else in life is going to perish, including this body in which I presently exist. Years later, after my mentor's death, her son asked me to speak at her funeral.

Miraculously, I could feel changes happening in those people who were present in her funeral attendance when I shared my mentor's lesson that had changed my life! I am still amazed how she directed me to conduct a 16 year, prison Bible Study Ministry. She was a remarkable woman.

I was excited to retire from work to be able to finally begin to have fun doing some things that I had previously never had time to do. I telephoned a High School classmate to ask if another classmate (that I knew had become a Physical Education Instructor) might be able to go rollerblading with me. Most people my age did not rollerblade. Subsequently, I had to always rollerblade with children. "It would be so wonderful to skate with an adult," I told my classmate. She informed me that the Phys-Ed classmate had recently had serious surgery and would not be able to skate at all. She then informed me of a world-wide, highly structured, 7 year Bible Study Fellowship program called, BSF-International. I thanked her for giving me such wonderful information; and I agreed that I would attend BSF with her now that I had time to become involved in such a serious study. "**You haven't been to <u>any</u> of our High School Class Reunions, Sarah** . . . A few of us get together, bring a dish to pass and meet in someone's back yard and laugh about old times. We have such a pot-luck scheduled at the end of this month . . . **Would you come?**" was her very definite question. As a favor to this friend, I said, "Yes!" **Immediately, I felt something <u>leaving</u> <u>my</u> <u>body</u>!** I had never prior, nor since felt that kind of strange feeling. I fell to my knees as soon as I hung up the telephone . . . "I didn't know anything like that was inside of me!" I exclaimed. "Anytime you won't have anything to do with someone, you have something against them." was the Lord's lesson. Wow, for 50 years (a half-century) I had not had anything to do with any of my old, High School classmates. Later, when I told my friend what had happened that day, she jokingly stated that, "Now I owe her really big-time!"

I learned more about the word of God in those seven years of BSF study than I had in a lifetime of regular church attendance. It was on 9/11 and I was in the sanctuary with our group of 525 students when the Church Secretary came in and informed our BSF Leader and group what had happened in New York City. Immediately we began to pray very seriously for all who were involved in the midst of that calamitous catastrophe, and their families; and our Nation. I was grateful to God to have been with the BSF women instead of being at home watching, while it happened on TV, and possibly crying while talking with someone on the telephone. Once I was at home, and I witnessed the repeat, TV broadcast of the individuals jumping from 97th floor windows in The Trade Center, I questioned the Lord. "Isn't it wrong to throw the gift of life back into the face of the Life-Giver? But there is a fireball rolling up behind us . . . What are we supposed to do?" I asked. "Ask ME for the sting," was HIS response. (I tried to understand what does that mean?) Then, I remembered the scripture that states . . . Death where is thy sting, O grave where is thy victory? I thought about the Hebrew Boys who were rescued from a fiery-furnace . . . and their clothes did not even smell like smoke! These lessons exemplify that believers in Christ do not have to live like non-believers; neither do they have to die like non-believers in Christ. Paul stated . . . To die is gain. Wow, if we live, we will work for Him; if we die, we will be with Him! This is a win/win lifestyle.

I now understand that when God told me to give up my prison, Bible Study Ministry and prepare my home to sell, it was to protect me from what later would become the "U.S., housing-market crisis." I was able to receive full value for that real estate. HE wanted me to go on the foreign mission field for Him. I was now living in an apartment building and although I was too old to live on the foreign mission field (with the Rafiki Foundation) therefore, I asked this BSF affiliate organization to send me to the East and West Coasts of Africa so that when I returned home I would be able to speak knowledgably about the Rafiki Foundation to raise money for their 10 Christian Villages within ten African Countries for the many millions of African orphans.

One morning in December of 2006, I was lying on the sofa in the living room in my apartment when I noticed a card next to my front door. I assumed it was a Christmas card. When I opened it, tears fell from my eyes because inside was a $50.00 gift from a woman who lived in the same building . . . I knew that money was half the amount of a Christmas gift that had been given to her by a relative. The card with it informed me that the money was for the orphans in Africa. I was emotional because I had not yet even traveled to Africa! "The prisoners in Michigan are going to bring money to the orphans in Africa," was what the Lord was telling me. "That does not compute? I do not understand what you mean?" was my question to Him. "You have been faithful to me in Jerusalem and Judea; now I am sending you to the uttermost parts of the earth," was His lesson. He let me know that the 16 years that I taught His word to prisoners was my training for what He had already convinced me to go on "a foreign mission assignment." I could not stop thanking Him for letting me have a glimpse of His Giant Plan. My trips to Kenya and Ghana are probably some of the most memorable and wonderful adventures within my lifetime, memory-bank. Those stories could be another book.

The following lesson began several years ago but culminated recently: One morning as I was getting out of bed, the Lord said to me, "you have known since you were a child (because it is scriptural) that God is love. If God is love, then Jesus is love; and if you are to be an imitator if Jesus, then you should want to be love, agape (unconditional) love. I want you to write a song about this lesson to share with others this message. What a day! This was the same day that my niece (an RN) was called to the hospital to help deliver the child she had been given permission to adopt. Our family had a double blessing that day. This little boy later had a prophecy on his life that he would become a "real man for God." Just recently, I should not have been, but I was shocked when this little boy (then in the third grade) was visiting me . . . and I learned what he was already able to recognize! I had him sitting in front of my computer to determine if he could understand a PowerPoint Presentation that I had put together for Middle School age students that might have difficulty understanding my book, *SMART IS AS SMART DOES, Emotional Self-control for Young People.* I asked him to read all of the positive and negative emotions (that we glanced at earlier in this book) and informed him that he should not worry if he could not pronounce all of those words. He began reading aloud most of the positive emotions so, when he came to some of the positive emotions that he did not recognize, I moved the film to the negative emotions section. He would not read them out loud; but he pointed to the screen with his finger and stated, "Aunt Sarah, Aunt Sarah, **this is sin**!" I thought I would fall from my chair . . . I was so shocked that **this 8 year old boy recognized what most adults do not even know!** It was the next day that the Lord informed me that when man was originally created, we were without sin; and that is why Adam and Eve had not recognized that they were both naked. This is the reason that we needed the Holy Spirit to help us to remove the negative emotions (that we take for granted) . . . so that we can live in the presence of a Holy God.

The television broadcast titled, *The Second Life* sounded as if I might enjoy it (I loved stories about individuals who went to heaven or hell) so I placed it on my TV record-system so that I could watch it when I had time to do so. Needless to say, I was surprised to learn that instead, it was information about the virtual, Internet World in which there is only Law against child-pornography. Permission has been granted that **everything else** is legal within *The Second Life*. Avatars (the vainly exaggerated, sexy cartoon character) are created by the millions of world viewers who participate to represent them, as they move around within this realm. Again, this old woman was shocked to learn about how everything that attracts humans in the real world is included within this fictional realm. There are Sex shops, dance halls (with naked, dancing avatars) beautiful clothes, homes, casinos, (even a stock market) and many games of sports. If you are raped, it does not matter, because an avatar cannot be hurt, nor can it conceive a baby. I immediately e-mailed my grandchildren to warn them about the misconceptions perpetuated by these concepts. The word of God lets us know that, "If a man <u>looks</u> upon a woman with lust within his heart, he has already committed the crime." That day, I mentioned this popular web-site to a minister (the father of young boys) to beware of this interesting game. He thanked me but, the woman who was hosting the minister's visit telephone me that evening and angrily informed me that what I discussed with her ministering guest was totally inappropriate. I tried to explain his appreciation of my information; she became so angry, she hung up the phone while I was speaking. The Lord let me know that anytime you take part of his rules and not all of his rules, you a self-righteous person and not a God-righteous person (one who obeys all of His rules.) I want you to write a song to explain this lesson . . . HE gave me the understanding of how our enemy, Satan uses the self-righteous people to work against the God-righteous people. HE said, "I want you to understand that what that woman who hung-up the telephone on you intended for your evil, I turned it into you good!" I thought how truly wonderful . . . my senior vocal group really loves this song. I want to share this God-given lesson with you. I have included this important message on the following page.

God-Righteous

Word and music by Sarah McChristian

CHORUS
I don't want to be self-righteous.
I want to be God-righteous. X2
And if I'm gonna' be God-righteous . . .
I've must be <u>completely</u> obedient to HIS word! (Whole section x2)

VERSE 1
Too many people pick their own "rights and wrongs."
So many people need to listen to this song.
Jesus said . . . "We can't live by bread alone."
Only every word from God takes us to HIS throne.
So if you wanna' be God-righteous. . .
You must not <u>ever</u> leave HIS Law alone!

VERSE 2
The Sadducees and Pharisees were certainly self-righteous.
The Enemy used <u>them</u> to fight the Jesus' righteousness.
Saul of Tarsus was self-righteous, that is (before he was struck down.)
But God does a one-eighty degrees, and turns all things around!
So if you wanna' be God-righteous. . .
Thank HIM for the <u>only</u> (existing) Law that is sound!

VERSE 3
Look at Peter and Judas; both men sorrowed at their sin.
Peter repented and was restored with faith again.
Judas was bitter . . . and committed a suicide end.
Jesus <u>gave</u> the examples to show <u>us</u> how to win!
So if you wanna' be God-righteous. . .
HIS Law you can <u>never, ever</u> bend!

I have truly been blessed to experience the wonderful opportunity to travel for our God. The most loving people that I have met on the planet are from the Underground Church in China. No one can say that there's is a ritualistic relationship with God. These Chinese people a willing to <u>risk their lives</u> to worship God in spirit and in truth. I have also learned that the people of Israel are very different from their leaders, as are we Americans. They were very loving and hospitable to me as a tourist. The wonderful bible took on a greater meaning for me when I was able to walk where Jesus had walked! The bible gives us the complete story. I placed God's Calendar near the end of the book to show how much bible prophecy has come to pass, so that we can recognize that whatever has **not** yet happened will happen exactly "to the letter."

BSF added another year of study to their program in 2010, so I was able to the study of the book of Isaiah for 32 weeks (which I had read 2 or 3 times prior) however; our lesson requirement was that we study several hundred old and new testament scriptures <u>related</u> to this book; so naturally, I have learned <u>more</u> in that year of study than I had previously by reading the entire book more than once. What a predictor of events in the future **God** is! I studied in chapters 41-44 (in the book of Isaiah) how He told Isaiah that Israel would be captured and taken into exile. However, a Persian King named Cyrus would rescue Israel and allow them to return home. Amazingly, these facts occurred within a period of 150 years **after** Isaiah's death! I love all of you who have taken time to read my experiences that have taught me truth. However, I don't believe in Christ only because of the writings of other people. I have a very intimate and personal loving relationship with the Lord, and have subsequently learned that <u>everything</u> He teaches me is in agreement with His word! My suggestion to non-believers in Christ is for them to just begin to look for <u>truth</u> by comparing the bible to History because . . . **History is HIS STORY!**

Last, but not least, for the very first time in my life, at Christmastime in 2010, the Lord gave me a Christmas Song to write, titled Love, Joy and Peace. My WinterGarden (senior vocal group) loved singing the new song along with our Christmas carols because beside the wonderful message, it has a wonderful bossa nova beat. Remember when I explained what the Lord taught me about the space within our emotional capacity in which nothing else fits? When we consider our accomplishments, our material assets or people as most important to us then we have become idolaters. Please do not become offended by the lyrics that the Lord gave me for this song because God understands our misunderstandings. (HE let me know that is how HE was so faithful to me when I was not faithful to HIM.) HE taught me that any family that does not teach their child about HIM prior to their leaving home to go out to school, is a dysfunctional family! (This is a completely different dysfunctional-family definition than is found in the field of Psychology.) Our Enemy, "The Prince of the power of the air" has much control outside our homes; as well as, what we grant to him inside our homes. God's lessons help us **if** we choose to follow them. HIS lessons hurt us if we ignore them. HE gives lessons to us to help us. (The bible lets us know that HIS WORD does not return unto HIM void. Isa. 55:11)

I pray that **all of my readers** will be blessed to experience a lifelong, most-precious, wonderful relationship with the King of Kings and Lord of Lords, in Jesus' name! Amen.

Love, Joy and Peace

Words and music by Sarah McChristian

CHORUS
Looking for love, joy and peace?
Then, look for Jesus!
He's the reason for the many, Christmas seasons . . .
HE is a gift from God to us! X2

VERSE
People look all over the world . . . for all three . . .
In dance halls, race tracks, stadiums and casinos (not for free!)
Get that money to buy houses, cars, clothes and jewelry!
Is that going to bring some prestige for me?

VERSE
People look in the wrong places . . . you see.
Their church is the movie theatre; their bible is the TV!
They want to look like, spend like, and _be_ like other celebrities!
We should all know that, that can never be!

VERSE
Put not your confidence in flesh!
Haven't your mistakes made a big enough mess?
Work for, to look forward to . . . being a co-heir with King Jesus! (for free!)
By learning His eternal, "**Kingdom Law of Love**" with **joy** and **peace**.

GOD'S CALENDAR

Time Dispensations Set Within Eternity

Goal= Ephesians 1:10

Old Testament _____ New Testament _____

Adam   Noah   Abraham

                                                    Moses   Christ

                                                               f
                                                               i
                                                               n
                                                               a
                                            King of Kings   l

                                    Death, burial,
                                    resurrection

                                            Kingdom
                                            Restoration

Eternity	1. Innocence	2. Conscience	3. Human Government	4 Promise	5. Law	Law Complete / Present / 6. Grace Church Age / Tribulation / 7 yrs	7. 1000 yrs.	Eternity
Glory	Garden							Glory

This Book is dedicated to Rosemary Jensen, the loving woman who established The Rafiki Foundation. This organization consist of 10 Christian, orphan villages in 10 different African countries. I have been blessed to visit and work with the Rafiki staff and children in Kenya and in Ghana (reason for the *Rafiki* Song) therefore, 50% of the profits from *The 2 of Me* will continually be dedicated to this remarkable organization.

THE RAFIKI SONG

Words & Music by Sarah McChristian

CHORUS (1 and 4)
  I want to help a friend (Yes!)
  I want to help Rafik!
  I want to help a friend (Praise God!)
  Because Jesus has truly helped me (Yes!)
2. I want to "Walk the Talk" (Yes!)
3. Until his Kingdom comes (Yes!)

VERSES

1. Out of the sinful world
  Some have come together
  To work a plan of God,
  To be for one another.

2. We've learned to "Walk the talk"
  Bind up the broken-hearted
  Provide for those who do not have
  Today we're being rewarded.

3. We'll show the world Agape love
  Until His kingdom comes
  A pleasure to be the Lord's hands and feet
  As teachers, uncles, aunties, and moms.

God is Love
Words and Music by Sarah McChristian

www.ingramcontent.com/pod-product-compliance
Lightning Source LLC
Chambersburg PA
CBHW081750280526
45789CB00008B/2808